# M A N U E L
# PONCE

# CONCIERTO

# DEL SUR

*FOR*

*GUITAR*

*AND*

*ORCHESTRA*

MUSIC MINUS ONE

3632

Music Minus One

3632

# CONTENTS

❖ ◆ ❖

# CONCIERTO DEL SUR

*Editing and fingering*
*by Christian Reichert*

Manuel M. Ponce

4

# Cadenza

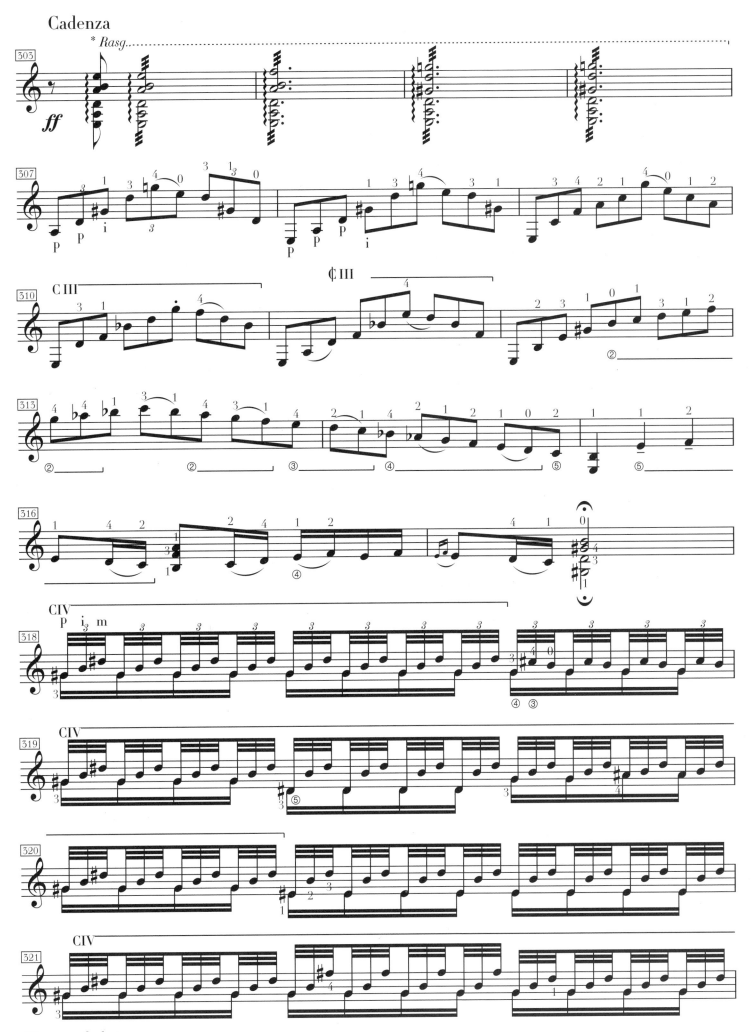

*Rasg: see the last page

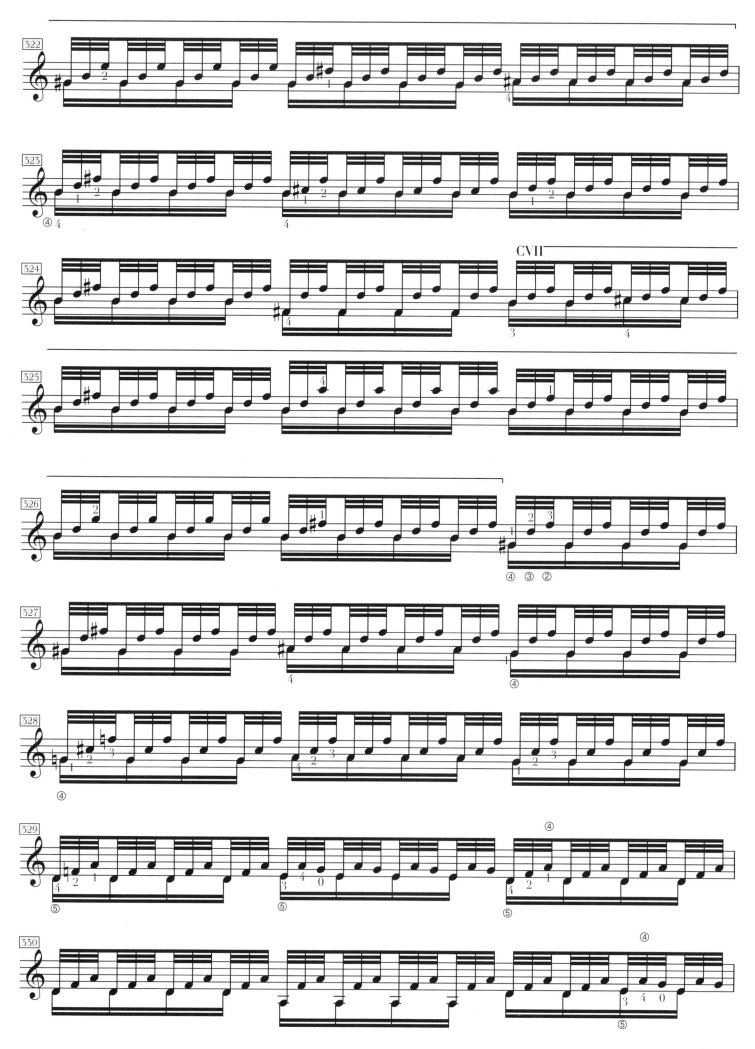

# II.

# III.

Engraving: Wieslaw Novak

# SUGGESTIONS FOR USING THIS MMO EDITION

**W**E HAVE TRIED to create a product that will provide you an easy way to learn and perform this concerto with a full orchestral accompaniment in the comfort of your own home. Because it involves a fixed accompaniment, there is an inherent lack of flexibility in tempo. The following mmo features and techniques will reduce these inflexibilities and help you maximize the effectiveness of the mmo practice and performance system:

Where either of the players begins *solo,* introductory taps have been provided on the accompaniments to help you set your pace. Also, track-breaks have been placed throughout each piece at appropriate practice sections, which will allow you to jump quickly throughout the score. Each of these track-breaks is cross-indexed in the score.

We have observed generally accepted tempi, but some may wish to perform at a different tempo, or to slow down or speed up the accompaniment for practice purposes. You can purchase from MMO specialized cd players and recorders which allow variable speed while maintaining proper pitch. This is an indispensable tool for the serious musician and you may wish to look into purchasing this useful piece of equipment for full enjoyment of all your MMO editions.

We want to provide you with the most useful practice and performance accompaniments possible. If you have any suggestions for improving the MMO system, please feel free to contact us. You can reach us by e-mail at *mmogroup@musicminusone.com.*

# PERFORMANCE NOTES

**I**f you want to play the *rasgueados* at the beginning of the Cadenza and in the last six bars of the third movement, you have to use the following technique: imagine that four thirty-second-notes are like one circle. I always start the circle with the thumb moving up (which means from the high strings to the low strings). The reason I start with the thumb is that it is the strongest finger, and so has to be the first of these four notes. The following three notes I do with the "a", "m" and "i" fingers in this order moving down (meaning from the low strings to the high strings). This should be practiced very slowly at the beginning and always having in mind that the right hand is not too tensioned and the moves are not too big. Only then can one make it to a proper speed.

In certain places I prefer Andrés Segovia's version of the *Concierto del Sur,* which he used in his concerts and his recording of the concerto. The concerto was written for him and he worked out the score very closely with Ponce. Some places differ from Ponce's first ideas, sounding much better and, ultimately, becoming established in the guitar world. In this matter I find it very interesting to read a short extract from a letter that Andrés Segovia wrote to Manuel Ponce after receiving his *Preludes*:

> *Certainly the preludes are not usable in the way in which they have been conceived.*
> *Most of them are of a difficulty which is incompatible with the character of elemen-*
> *tary studies which is given to them by the scale which precedes each one; and some*
> *of them are totally impossible.*

This quotation should not put down Ponce's status as a composer. But it makes clear how much he worked together with Segovia and appreciated his opinion. And we as guitarists should not stick like glue to every note, but rather try to find the music between the notes.

Christian Reichert
Freiburg (Germany)
November 2005

## MUSIC MINUS ONE
50 Executive Boulevard
Elmsford, New York 10523-1325
800.669.7464 U.S. ← 914.592.1188 International

www.musicminusone.com
mmogroup@musicminusone.com

MMO 3632                    Pub. No. 00353                    Printed in Canada